SCIENCE
QUESTIONS & ANSWERS

Plant Science

Anita Ganeri

Evans

Published by Evans Brothers Limited
2A Portman Mansions
Chiltern Street
London W1M 1LE

First published 1993

Printed in Hong Kong by Wing King Tong Co., Ltd.

ISBN 0 237 51246 7

Acknowledgements

The author and publishers would like to thank the following for her valuable help and advice:
Sally Morgan MA, MSc, MIBiol

Illustrations: Virginia Gray
Editors: Catherine Chambers and Jean Coppendale
Design: Monica Chia
Production: Jenny Mulvanny

For permission to reproduce copyright material the author and publishers gratefully acknowledge the following:
Cover photographs: (top left) Saguaro Cactus, Arizona, USA, John Lythgoe, Planet Earth Pictures, (bottom left) Venus fly trap,
Stephen Dalton, NHPA, (main photograph) Mr P Clement, Bruce Coleman Limited, (bottom right) Bladderwrack seaweed,
Laurie Campbell, NHPA.
Page 8 – Ken Lucas, Planet Earth Pictures; page 9 – (left) Sally Morgan, Ecoscene, (right) Dr Eckart Pott, Bruce Coleman Limited; page
10 – Schaffer, Ecoscene; page 12 – (left) E & D Hosking, Frank Lane Picture Agency, (top right) E & D Hosking, Frank Lane Picture
Agency, (bottom right) E & D Hosking, Frank Lane Picture Agency; page 13 – Andrew D R Brown, Ecoscene; page 14 – Hans Reinhard,
Bruce Coleman Limited; page 15 – (top) Tweedie, Ecoscene, (bottom) Anthony King; page 16 – Sally Morgan, Ecoscene; page 17 –
(left) Kloske, Ecoscene, (right) Nicholls, Ecoscene; page 20 – Robert Tyrrell, Oxford Scientific Films; page 21 – (top) Heather Angel,
(bottom) Harry Fox, Oxford Scientific Films; page 22 – Jane Burton, Bruce Coleman Limited; page 24 – (top) Sally Morgan, Ecoscene,
(bottom) WWF/Timm Rautert, Bruce Coleman Limited; page 25 – (left) Brian Rogers, Heather Angel, (right) Heather Angel; page 26
– Chris Prior, Planet Earth Pictures; page 27 – Heather Angel; page 28 – (left) Jane Burton, (right) Marie Read, Bruce Coleman Limited;
page 29 – (left) MWF Tweedie, NHPA, (right) Sally Morgan, Ecoscene; page 30 – Dr G S Grant, Oxford Scientific Films; page 31 – (top)
Ken Lucas, Planet Earth Pictures, (bottom) Anthony King; page 32 – Paul Ormerod, Heather Angel; page 33 – (inset) Peter Stevenson,
Planet Earth Pictures, (top) John Anthony, Bruce Coleman Limited, (bottom) Ian Harwood, Ecoscene; page 34 – (left) L Campbell,
NHPA, (right) Patrick Clement, Bruce Coleman Limited; page 35 – (left) Tom Leach, Oxford Scientific Films, (top right) Andrew
Mounter, Planet Earth Pictures, (bottom right) Andrew Mounter, Planet Earth Pictures; page 36 – (main picture) P J Herring, Heather
Angel, (inset) Oxford Scientific Films; page 37 – (top) Heather Angel, (bottom) Doug Allan, Oxford Scientific Films; page 38 – (left)
Dave Jacobs, Robert Harding Picture Library, (top right) Ecoscene, (bottom right) Sally Morgan, Ecoscene; page 39 – (top left) M
Newman, Frank Lane Picture Agency, (bottom left) Sally Morgan, Ecoscene, (right) Sally Morgan, Ecoscene; page 40 – (main picture)
Gryniewicz, Ecoscene, (inset) Heather Angel; page 41 – (left) Breck P Kent, Oxford Scientific Films, (right) Patrick Clements, Bruce
Coleman Limited; page 43 – (top) J & G Lythgoe, Planet Earth Pictures, (bottom) Mark Mattock, Planet Earth Pictures; page 44 – ZEFA;
page 45 – Gryniewicz, Ecoscene.

Contents

What types of plant are there? 6
- Flowering plants
- Non-flowering plants
- How are plants different from animals?

When did plants first grow on Earth? 8
- What were the first forests like?
- What were the first flowers like?

Why are plants green? 10
- How do plants make their food?
- Why do plants have leaves?

Why do some trees change colour in autumn? 12
- What does 'evergreen' mean?

How do plants help you to breathe? 14
- How do plants breathe?

Why do plants have roots? 16
- Which plants have roots that grow in the air?

Why do leaves have 'veins'? 18
- How does water travel around a plant?

Why do plants have flowers? 20
- Why do flowers smell?
- What do petals do?
- Which flowers look like insects?

How do plants make seeds? 22
- How do seeds grow into new plants?
- Which plants grow the fastest?
- Which plants grow the slowest?
- Which is the biggest plant?

What types of fruit are there? 26
- Which other parts of a plant can you eat?

What is the difference between fruit and vegetables?
- Which fruits can you wash with?

Which plants eat meat? 28
- Which plants smell like meat?
- Which plants live off other plants?

How do trees grow? 30
- How can you tell the age of a tree?

Why do trees have bark? 32
- Why does bark make different patterns?
- Where does cork come from?

How do plants protect themselves? 34
- How do plants survive the cold?
- Which plant has collapsing leaves?
- Which plants glow in the dark?
- Which plants look like pebbles?

How can desert plants live without water? 38
- Why do cacti have spines?
- Why do some deserts suddenly burst into flower?

What is seaweed? 40
- Which plants can forecast the weather?
- Which plants can test pollution?

What are fungi? 42
- What is the difference between mushrooms and toadstools?

How do people use plants? 44
- How is paper made?

Glossary 46
Further reading 46
Index 47

What types of plant are there?

Scientists who study plants are called botanists. They think that there are over 375,000 different species, or types, of plant in the world. Plants come in all sizes. There are tiny algae made of just one **cell**, which live mainly in water and look like little green blobs, and there are towering trees, taller than houses. Plants range in shape from fern **fronds** and seaweed strands, to orchids that look like bees. These plants develop and grow all over the world, and in very different **environments**, from the coldest, windiest mountain slopes to the steamiest jungles.

To make plants easier to study, botanists have divided them into different groups. These are based on what a plant looks like, whether or not it has flowers, and how the plant grows. You can see how these groups work below.

Flowering plants

This is by far the biggest group of plants. It has about 250,000 species. The plants in this group produce flowers. They include poppies, daisies, grasses, shrubs, and trees such as horse chestnut and cherry trees.

Non-flowering plants

These are plants which do not produce proper flowers. There are several different groups of them.

Algae are very simple plants, with no proper leaves, roots or flowers. They grow in water or damp places. Some algae are smaller than full stops. You can only see them under a microscope. Seaweeds are the biggest types of algae (see pages 40 and 41).

Mosses and liverworts are simple plants which like to live in damp places. They have no proper roots or flowers. They do not grow from seeds as some plants do, but from **spores**.

Ferns and horsetails also grow from spores, not from seeds. Ferns are tough plants which can grow quite tall because they have strong stems.

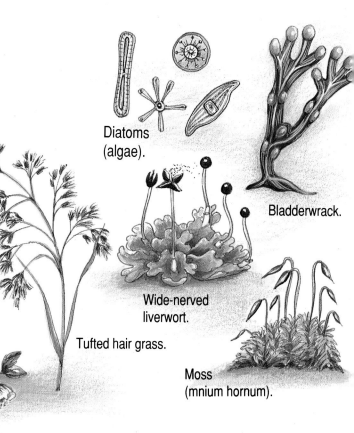

Diatoms (algae).

Bladderwrack.

Wide-nerved liverwort.

Tufted hair grass.

Moss (mnium hornum).

Cherry blossom (prunus pandora).

Did you know?

There is no difference between plants and trees. A tree is simply a type of plant with a thick, woody stem which we call a trunk. Trees are taller than most other plants. There are three groups of trees – broad-leaved trees, conifers and palms (see pages12 and 13).

Fungi include toadstools, mushrooms and moulds. They are so strange that some botanists do not think that they are plants at all (see pages 42 and 43).

Lichens are mixtures of algae and fungi. In lichens, the algae and the fungi cannot survive without each other's help. There are many different kinds of lichen. Look out for them growing in crusts on walls or rocks. Leafier lichens sometimes grow on the bark of trees, and on walls.

Conifers are trees, such as pine, fir and redwood trees. They have cones instead of flowers and fruit.

How are plants different from animals?

There are many differences between plants and animals. But the most important ones are to do with how they get their food. Animals have to move around and search for their food. This is what you are doing when you go to the supermarket. But plants stay in one place all the time, and most of them can make their own food (see pages 10 and 11). There are some sea animals, such as sponges and corals, which do not move either, but they have to get their food from the water around them as they cannot make it for themselves.

Some animals disguise themselves as plants to avoid being seen and eaten by their enemies. Similarly, it is useful for some plants to look like animals.

Velvet shank fungus.

Lichen.

Common horsetail.

Bracken (fern).

Douglas fir.

Monterey pine.

When did plants first grow on Earth?

The first plants that ever lived were tiny sea plants with just one cell, very much like the algae which we have today. They lived about 3,000 million years ago, long before the first animals appeared. Plants did not start to live on land until about 400 million years ago. They were probably sea plants that had been stranded when the tide went out, or when the pool of water in which they lived, dried up. These plants then **adapted** to life on land.

The first land plant we know of was called Cooksonia. It was like a short type of grass, but it only had shoots, with no leaves, flowers or proper roots. At first, plants grew quite low to the ground. But as more types of plants developed, they had to fight for their share of space and sunlight. So they grew taller. This meant that they needed strong stems and deep roots for support.

What were the first forests like?

The first forests were swampy, steamy jungles filled with plants such as clubmosses, horsetails and ferns. Horsetails and ferns grow today, but in prehistoric times they were much taller, sometimes as tall as trees are now. In fact, some giant horsetails grew over 45 metres high. How many metres tall are you?

This is probably what a steamy prehistoric swamp looked like about 300 million years ago.

This fossilized fern grew 300 million years ago.

These plants covered large parts of the Earth about 345 to 280 million years ago, before the dinosaurs lived. This was called the Carboniferous period, which means 'coal-bearing'. When the plants died, they fell into the swamps and gradually were buried under more plants and rocks. Over many millions of years, the weight of the rocks squeezed the water out of the plants and they turned into coal. Coal-miners sometimes find fossils of prehistoric plants inside lumps of coal.

The first trees lived about 300 million years ago. Scientists have studied fossils of them, and think that they were probably types of pine and spruce tree (see page 13).

 Did you know?

The oldest tree alive today is a bristlecone pine growing in the White Mountains of California, in the USA. It is 4,700 years old. But it is not the oldest plant that we know. Some scientists think that lichens growing in the Antarctic may be 10,000 years old.

This is a wind-battered bristlecone pine.

What were the first flowers like?

The first flowering plants lived about 100 million years ago, towards the end of the dinosaur age. The oldest flower fossils found so far were of magnolia flowers. They looked very much like magnolia flowers today. Other early flowering plants looked like waterlilies.

No one is sure why the dinosaurs died out about 65 million years ago. But some say that they were poisoned by the first flowering plants.

Some of the first flowers looked very like these waterlilies.

 Did you know?

In 1954, scientists found an Arctic lupin seed buried in the frozen ground in Canada. It was about 10,000 years old. But it still sprouted and grew into a new plant when the scientists planted it.

Why are plants green?

Most plants have green leaves. This is because they contain a special green pigment, or colouring, called chlorophyll. Just under the top surface of the leaves is a layer of special cells, known as palisade cells. Inside each there are tiny disc-shaped containers, called chloroplasts. These are full of chlorophyll.

How do plants make their food?

Plants need plenty of sunlight, water and air to make their own food. During the day, the chlorophyll in the plants' leaves absorbs, or takes in, light from the sun. The plant uses this to turn carbon dioxide from the air, and water from the ground, into a sugary food. Plants give off oxygen as a waste product, although some is used for breathing (see page 15). This process is

These leaves are opened out to catch as much sunlight as possible.

called photosynthesis. The food can be stored inside the plants and used when it is needed.

Animals and people take advantage of plants' ability to make their own food. They eat many plant species and plant food stores as well (see pages 26 and 45).

Section through a leaf

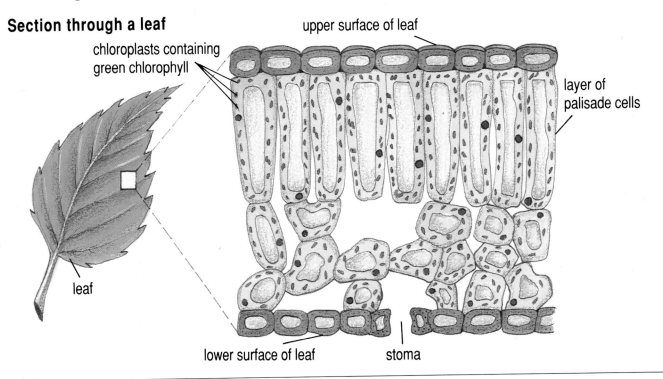

chloroplasts containing green chlorophyll

upper surface of leaf

layer of palisade cells

leaf

lower surface of leaf

stoma

10

Why do plants have leaves?

Leaves come in a huge variety of sizes and shapes, from pine-needles to palm fronds and from waterlily pads to oak leaves. But they all have the same main purpose – to make food. Leaves are arranged on the plant's stem in a special way, so that each leaf traps as much sunlight as possible. Plants also breathe through their leaves (see page 15) and lose water through them (see page 19).

Banana palm.

Oak.

Scots pine.

Waterlily.

(see page 15)
(see page 19)

 ## See for yourself

Plants will always try to grow towards the light, because without light a plant cannot photosynthesize. You can prove this with houseplants. Stand a houseplant on a sunny window-ledge and watch it over the next week or so. See how the plant leans towards the sun to get as much light as possible.

 ## Did you know?

The raffia palm has leaves almost 20 metres long – over 30 times longer than one of your arms. An oak tree may have over 250,000 leaves.

 ## See for yourself

If there is a pond near your home, collect some pond-water in a clean jam jar. The water should look quite clear at first. Stand the jar in a sunny place and watch it for a week or two. It should turn green quite quickly as the tiny, **microscopic** algae in the water photosynthesize and multiply.

1. Quite clear pond-water.   *2. The algae have turned the water green.*

Why do some trees change colour in autumn?

The countryside looks a very different place in the autumn. The leaves of trees such as beeches, oaks and sycamores change from summer green to rich red, russet and gold. Then they fall off the trees as winter comes.

These are called deciduous trees. They are mostly broad-leaved trees, such as the ones mentioned above. Their leaves are usually quite large, and the trees produce flowers and fruit in summer and autumn.

The leaves start to die in autumn, and this is when they change colour. The green chlorophyll breaks down and is stored in the plant until spring. This allows other pigments, or colourings, in the leaves to show through.

In winter, these trees lose their leaves so that they can survive the cold weather. Their roots find it difficult to suck up enough water from the frozen ground to supply the whole tree, leaves and all. So the leaves dry up, die and fall off the tree. New leaves grow the following spring, in the warmer weather. During the summer, the rich reds and yellows of the new leaves are hidden by the green chlorophyll, which helps the tree to make food.

Top: In summer, a beech tree's branches are covered in green leaves.
Top right: The beech tree's leaves begin to change colour as autumn arrives.
Right: In winter, the tree's branches are bare. All its leaves have died and fallen off.

What does 'evergreen' mean?

Some trees are evergreen. This means that their leaves stay green all year round and do not fall off in winter. Evergreen trees are usually conifers, such as pine, fir and spruce. They have thin, tough needles and cones, instead of large leaves, flowers and fruit. This is why they are also called coniferous trees.

Conifers often grow in very cold, windswept places. Their needles and their conical shapes help them to survive. The needles are coated in wax, which stops them from drying out in the cold wind. The trees' sloping branches allow snow to slide off, so that it does not form heavy piles and snap off the branches. Most conifers keep the same leaves for up to four years.

Spruce and sub-alpine fir trees surround a lake in Revelstoke Park, Canada.

 See for yourself

Keep a nature diary and note down any changes that you see in the trees around you from one season to the next. Visit the same tree at the same time of day once a month. Write down as many details as you can. Does the tree have buds or leaves? What colour are the leaves? Can you see any flowers or fruit? Are there any animals or other plants living in or near the tree? Try sketching the trees at each stage, or even take photographs.

 Did you know?

The biggest forest in the world is a conifer forest stretching across the far north of Russia. This one forest makes up a quarter of all the forest land on Earth.

How do plants help you to breathe?

When plants photosynthesize, they give off oxygen as waste. This is the gas which all plants and animals, including people, need to breathe to stay alive. Without plants, there would not be enough oxygen in the air for us to be able to survive.

When plants first appeared on Earth millions of years ago, there were no animals. The air was thick with poisonous gases such as methane and ammonia, but no oxygen. Gradually the plants put enough oxygen into the air for animals to develop and survive.

Water plants are also important. They put oxygen into the water. The

 Did you know?

The first oxygen-making plants on Earth were algae, which lived in the prehistoric seas. Sea algae still produce over 70 per cent of all the oxygen in the air.

oxygen dissolves in the water and is then breathed by fish and other water creatures.

When people and animals breathe, carbon dioxide is produced as waste. This is used by plants to help make their food.

Here you can see a pond surrounded by plants. It also has algae and waterlilies growing on its surface.

How do plants breathe?

Plants need to breathe just like animals and people. During the day, as well as giving out oxygen, plants also use oxygen and give out carbon dioxide just as you do when you breathe (see page 10). They are able to make their own food, but like you, they have to break it down into energy by breathing, or respiration. This energy is used for growing and repairing worn-out tissue. At night, when plants cannot photosynthesize, they have to take in oxygen from the air outside. In this way, they can carry on breathing.

Plants do not have lungs like you, or gills like fish. The gases from the air pass through tiny holes underneath their leaves. These holes are called stomata. You can read about what else they do on page 19. Plants that live underwater need to 'breathe' the oxygen which is dissolved in the water.

At dawn and dusk, a plant's photosynthesis and respiration happen

Seaweeds breathe through tiny holes on their fronds.

at the same speed. They balance each other out, so the plant is making and breaking down its food at the same rate. This means that the plant does not have to take in extra ingredients from the air around it. At most other times, one process happens faster than the other.

 See for yourself

The oxygen made by plants usually vanishes into the air. You cannot normally see it. But try putting some pondweed or waterweed into a clear, clean bowl of water and standing it in the sun for a while. You should soon see tiny bubbles of oxygen coming from the weed.

The tiny bubbles on this pondweed (Elodea crispa) will eventually rise to the surface of the water.

Why do plants have roots?

A plant needs a firm base in the ground, just like a building, so that it is not blown over by the wind. Its roots are like anchors, holding it down in the soil. But they have another very important job to do. Roots take in water and minerals from the ground, which the plant needs to make its food.

The roots of some plants grow very deep into the soil. But most roots branch out over a wider, more shallow area. This gives them a firmer base and a larger patch of ground for collecting water and minerals.

[?] Did you know?

The deepest plant roots known belong to a wild fig-tree growing at Echo Caves in South Africa. Its roots measure 120 metres, about as long as 1,000 medium-sized carrots.

Parts of a root system

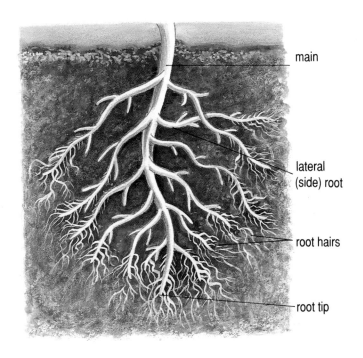

main

lateral (side) root

root hairs

root tip

The force of gravity makes roots grow deep down into the soil.

Storm-blown beech tree showing base and roots.

Which plants have roots that grow in the air?

Some plants have very odd roots indeed. In the tropical rainforests, there are orchids that live high up on the branches of tall trees. They have roots that dangle in the air. These are called aerial roots. It is very humid and sticky in the rainforest. The air contains a lot of **water vapour**. The orchids' aerial roots take in the water which they need, from the air.

Other rainforest trees have extra roots, called buttress roots, growing out of their trunks. The roots take in extra water and **nutrients** from the rain which runs down the trunks.

Mangrove trees live in the estuaries of some tropical rivers, where the river flows into the sea. As well as normal roots, they use roots growing from their trunks to hold them firmly in the soft mud. These roots are called stilt roots.

These mangrove trees are firmly anchored by their stilt roots.

Some rainforest trees have huge buttress roots growing out of their trunks.

 See for yourself

You can see how plants develop roots by growing your own cuttings. Fill some clean jam jars with about 5 centimetres of lukewarm water. Cut off some lengths of stem from plants such as geraniums or bizzy-lizzies. They should be about 10 centimetres long. Put the cuttings in the water and leave them for a week or so. They should soon grow some roots. Then you can plant them in pots filled with **potting compost**. Water the plants well and leave them to grow.

Why do leaves have 'veins'?

Next time you go outside, pick up different kinds of leaves and look at the pattern of veins on their surface. The veins are part of a plant's transport system. Together with the roots and the tubes inside the stem, they carry water, minerals and food around the plant.

There are two networks of tubes inside a plant. They are called xylem and phloem. The xylem carry water and minerals from the roots to the leaves, where they are needed to help make food. The phloem carry food, in the form of sticky sap, from the leaves to the other parts of the plant. The tubes act like the veins and arteries inside you, which carry blood around your body.

The veins of plants also act as skeletons. They help to make the leaves stronger and give them their shape. Some leaves have branching veins. Others have long, **parallel** veins. Botanists use the vein patterns to help them **identify** different types of plant.

⚠ See for yourself

A good way of looking more closely at a leaf's vein pattern is to take a leaf rubbing. Place your leaf on a piece of thick card, then cover it with a piece of thin white paper. Rub gently over the paper with a soft pencil to make the veins show through.

This leaf rubbing is of a horse chestnut leaf. Try making a picture with lots of different types of leaves.

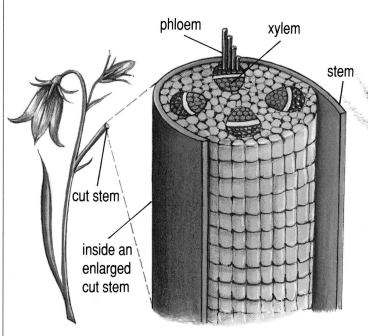

The cut stem has been enlarged to show the xylem and phloem inside.

phloem   xylem   stem

cut stem

inside an enlarged cut stem

How does water travel around a plant?

A plant's roots suck up water from the ground, then the xylem tubes carry it up the stem to the leaves. The leaves use some of the water to make food. But some also escapes through the tiny holes, called stomata, underneath the leaves (see page 15). This loss of water is called transpiration.

The water then evaporates from the leaves into the air. This means that it turns from liquid water into invisible water vapour. On hot days, the rate of evaporation is faster that on cold days. If leaves lose too much water, they shrivel up and die. So the stomata do not stay open all the time, especially in very hot weather. They open so that gases can pass in and out of the plant for photosynthesis and respiration (see pages 10, 14 and 15). But the stomata can close if the plant is losing too much water.

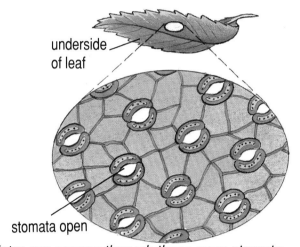

underside of leaf

stomata open

Water can escape through these open stomata.

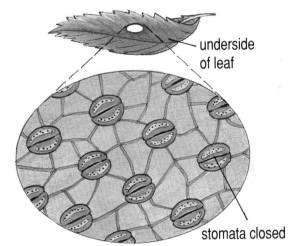

underside of leaf

stomata closed

These stomata are closed to stop the leaf losing too much water.

⚠️ See for yourself

Try this experiment to see how water travels up through a plant. Take a white, or very light-coloured carnation with a long stem. Slice through the bottom section of the stem. Fill two drinking glasses with water. Add a few drops of food colouring to one of them. Stand the carnation with half its stem in each glass and support it against a wall or window. After about 30 minutes you should see half the flower begin to change colour as the food dye reaches it.

Why do plants have flowers?

Each plant needs to reproduce, or create new plants, so that its species survives. Many plants have flowers so that seeds can be made inside them. These seeds will eventually grow into new plants.

Flowers contain the plants' male and female parts. They are both needed to make seeds. Some flowers have both male and female parts in the same flower. Others have either one or the other.

The male parts make a fine, powdery dust called pollen. This is what makes you sneeze if you get hay fever. To make a seed, pollen has to travel from the male parts to join with the female parts. This is called pollination. It does not usually happen in the same flower, even if this flower contains both male and female parts. Pollen has to be taken from the male part of one flower

The parts of a flower

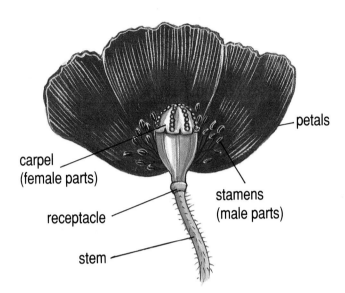

This is a section through a poppy flower.

to the female part of another. But plants cannot move about, so how does the pollen get there?

Plants have several helpers to transport their pollen. They use the wind, which blows pollen from one flower to another. They also use the services of animals such as bees, butterflies, bats and birds. But first they have to tempt the animals to visit them.

Why do flowers smell?

A flower's shape, colour and smell are designed to attract animals to help pollinate it. It also has a sweet syrup deep inside, called nectar, which animals like to eat. The animals visit the flower and get covered in pollen dust as they feed. When they fly off to another flower, some of the pollen

In the tropics, hummingbirds use their long beaks to reach the nectar inside flowers.

A bumblebee gets covered in pollen as it searches for nectar on this dahlia flower.

brushes off. If it brushes onto the female parts, a seed may grow.

Catkins and other flowers that use the wind to pollinate them are dull and drab. They do not need to tempt animals to visit them. But flowers such as honeysuckle, cherry blossom, pansies and sunflowers use sweet smells and bright petals to attract insects for pollination.

What do petals do?

Plants use brightly-coloured petals to attract insects, as we have seen. Some petals have dark markings on them, called honeyguides. These are thought

The dark honeyguides show up clearly on the pansies' yellow petals.

to guide insects to the flower's store of nectar deep inside the flower. Other petals, such as those on foxglove flowers, are shaped to make sure that insects pollinate them. They have a good landing platform on the outside. Their tight bell shape makes insects, such as bumblebees, force their way inside. The bees cannot avoid getting coated with pollen as they tunnel their way through to the nectar. Petals also help to protect the flower's male and female parts.

Which flowers look like insects?

Some tropical orchids use disguises to attract flies, wasps and bees for pollination. Their flowers look like female insects. They even smell like them, and their petals look like the insects' furry bodies. The disguises are so life-like that male insects visit the flowers and try to mate with them. In the process they get coated with pollen dust, which they carry to the next flower that they visit. The bee orchid, which you can see on the title page, is a good example of a flower that looks like an insect.

 Did you know?

The world's biggest flower is the Rafflesia. It grows in the jungles of south-east Asia. Its flower can measure a metre across, which is wider than a car tyre. The smallest flowering plant is a type of duckweed called Wolffia. Over 30 of these plants would fit across the head of a drawing pin.

How do plants make seeds?

When a flower has been pollinated, a male pollen grain joins with the female part of the flower to make a seed. This will eventually grow into a new plant. But first it has to be carried away from its parent plant so that there is not too much competition for space, light, water and nutrients.

A plant needs help to spread its seeds, just as a flower needs help to spread its pollen. Dandelion and sycamore seeds are light enough to be blown away by the wind. They also have special shapes to help them fly.

Prickly burrs contain burdock seeds. They get caught on the coats of dogs and foxes and are carried in this way. Birds enjoy a tasty meal of sweet berries or cherries. Then the seeds inside them pass through the birds and are spread in their droppings.

Other plants, such as laburnum trees, have pods that burst open and shoot the seeds out. If these seeds land in a sunny place with good soil, they will grow into new plants. Laburnum seeds are very poisonous to us, as are many berries.

How do seeds grow into new plants?

Inside a seed there is a food store, and the parts which will grow into a new plant. The young plant lives off this store of food until its leaves are big enough to make their own food. If the seed lands in a good patch of moist soil, its case splits open and the first, small root digs into the soil to anchor it. Then its first shoot appears. Gradually the roots and shoots grow bigger and stronger, and the new plant's leaves grow. This process is called germination.

The dandelion's yellow flower becomes a fluffy seedhead. The slightest breeze will blow the seeds away.

Did you know?

The biggest seeds come from the coco-de-mer palm. This rare plant only grows on the Seychelle Islands in the Indian Ocean. One of its huge seeds may weigh 18 kilograms, as much as 160 apples. Orchids make the smallest seeds. It would take over 560 million orchid seeds to weigh as much as just one apple.

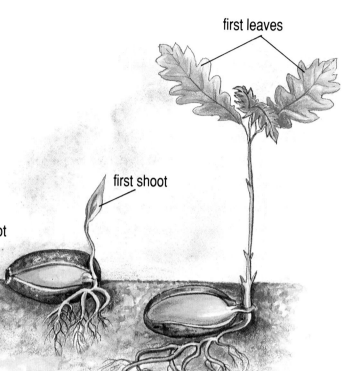

first leaves

first shoot

first root

acorn

Here you can see how an acorn grows into a young oak tree.

See for yourself

Try growing your own plants from seed. Collect some apple or orange pips. Soak them in water overnight. Find some old yoghurt or margarine pots and punch a few small drainage holes in the bottom. Put a layer of small stones in the bottom and fill the pots with compost. Then plant a few pips in each tub, cover them with a little more compost, and water them well. Cover each pot with a plastic bag, held in place with an elastic band. Keep the pots in a warm place, away from direct sunlight, until the shoots appear. Then take off the plastic bags, move the tubs to a sunnier place and watch your plants grow. When the plants get bigger you will need to replant them in larger pots.

plastic bag

elastic band

orange pips

yoghurt pot   small stones

The small stones in the bottom of the pot allow water to drain through, so the soil does not get waterlogged.

Which plants grow the fastest?

Some plants grow very fast indeed. The Pacific giant kelp, the longest type of seaweed, can grow at a rate of 45 centimetres a day. But it stops growing when its strands reach a length of 45 metres. Some types of bamboo grow twice as fast, at 90 centimetres a day.

Bamboo is the favourite food of giant pandas in China. Today, these pandas are very rare because there is not enough food for them. This is partly because of the strange way in which the bamboo grows. It only flowers and produces seeds once every 100 years. Then it dies. In the past, this did not cause any problems. The pandas simply moved to another patch of the forest. But today people have cut down so much of the forest to clear the land, that the pandas have nowhere to go. Many of them starve.

 Did you know?

Albizzia trees like the one below are members of the pea family. They all grow very fast. The fastest growing variety is Albizzia falcata. One of these grew 10.74 metres in just 13 months. If you grew at this rate you would be as tall as a 30-storey building by the time you were ten years old!

Giant pandas feed in the bamboo forests of China.

Which plants grow the slowest?

The slowest-growing tree, the Dioon edule, only grows 0.7 millimetres a year. One of these trees measured just under 10 centimetres, even though it was 150 years old.

The Puya raimondii plant is the slowest plant of all to produce flowers. It grows high up in the mountains in South America. It does not flower until it is between 80 and 150 years old. Then it grows a flower spike, taller than three people. This is covered in as many as 8,000 small white flowers. The plant dies after it has flowered. The Puya raimondii is the biggest type of herb, the strong-smelling group of plants which includes parsley, basil and thyme. They are often used in cooking or for making medicines.

This gigantic flower spike of the Puya raimondii grows in Peru.

Which is the biggest plant?

'General Sherman' is the world's biggest plant and the largest living thing on Earth.

A giant sequoia tree, nicknamed 'General Sherman' after a great American soldier, is the biggest plant in the world. In fact it is the biggest thing that has ever lived on Earth, even larger than the huge blue whale. The tree stands in Sequoia National Park in California, USA. It is over 83 metres tall, taller than 15 giraffes, and measures over 25 metres around its trunk. How much do you measure around your waist? How does this measurement compare with the tree trunk? 'General Sherman' weighs an amazing 2,500 tonnes, more than 400 elephants. It is thought to have enough wood to make 5 billion matchsticks!

What types of fruit are there?

Fruits grow around a plant's seeds to protect them and to help them get scattered. Many fruits are also delicious to eat. They come in many shapes and sizes. Fruits include berries, nuts, and pods such as those which cover peas or beans. There are also apples, dates and plums. The 'keys' that spin away from sycamore trees are also fruits. Conifers have cones that do the same job as other fruits. They open in warm weather to release the seeds which they contain. Exotic fruits include pineapples, coconuts and pomegranates.

Which other parts of a plant can you eat?

People have collected plants to eat since prehistoric times. Apart from fruits, we eat many other parts of a plant. Carrots and radishes are roots. Beans and peas are seeds. We also eat many stems and stalks, such as celery.

Some plants die down in winter. Only their underground parts, such as bulbs and tubers, survive. A bulb is a short, thick stem covered in dry, scaly leaves. Bulbs form from the base of leaves around the plant's stem. The stem becomes swollen with a store of food

This fruit market in Indonesia sells delicious tropical fruits, such as papaya, guava and jackfruit.

supplied by the dying leaves above ground. The plant lives off this store through the winter, until a new shoot grows again from the bulb when spring arrives. Onions and garlic are types of bulb that we eat. Plants such as daffodils, tulips and hyacinths make bulbs as well.

Tubers are also stores of food. They are short, swollen underground stems. Tubers have buds on them that grow into new plants. Potatoes and yams are types of tuber.

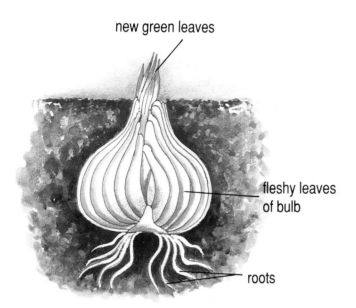

new green leaves

fleshy leaves of bulb

roots

This is a section through an onion bulb.

What is the difference between fruit and vegetables?

Is a tomato a fruit or a vegetable? What do you think? We often think of it as a vegetable. But it is really a fruit because it grows around seeds to protect them. We seem to call things vegetables if they have a savoury taste, rather than a sweet, fruity one. Roots, stems and leaves are used as vegetables, as well as some fruits.

Which fruit can you wash with?

Do you use a loofah to scrub your back with in the bath? It looks a bit like a sponge. But unlike a sponge, it does not come from the sea and is not an animal. It is actually the fruit of a plant like a marrow. The ripe fruits are picked and soaked in water until their outer cases break up. The remaining parts are dried and **bleached** to give them a light colour. These are the loofahs which you can buy.

These loofahs are being dried in the sun.

 Did you know?

The longest carrot ever grown measured 4.9 metres. This is almost as long as three bicycles standing end to end.

 Did you know?

The avocado is very good for you. It is the most **nourishing** fruit in the world. Avocados are ten times more nutritious than cucumbers, which are refreshing but have very little goodness in them.

Which plants eat meat?

Some plants can make their own food by photosynthesis – but they also eat meat. This is because they often live in boggy places where the soil is not very rich in the minerals which they need. The meat provides them with extra nourishment. These meat-eating plants are called carnivorous plants. They include Venus fly-traps, pitcher plants and bladderworts.

The Venus fly-trap has leaves which are hinged together. They lie wide open, waiting for insects to come and land on their colourful surfaces. Then they snap shut, trapping the insect inside. The plant dissolves the insect's body with special **digestive juices,** and then **absorbs** the liquid. Insects such as dragonflies are the Venus fly-trap's usual victims, but animals as large as frogs have been found inside them. It takes the plant about two weeks to digest a dragonfly.

Pitcher plants have amazing pitcher, or jug-shaped, leaves complete with lids to keep the rain out. Insects are tempted to visit this plant by the stores of sweet nectar under the lids, and around the rim of the pitcher. But the walls of the pitcher are very slippery.

A bluebottle is about to be trapped inside the Venus fly-trap's leaves.

Insects are lying in the bottom of this pitcher plant, about to be digested.

As soon as an insect lands, it loses its footing and slides down into a pool of liquid at the bottom of the pitcher. It cannot get out, and drowns.

Bladderworts live in ponds and lakes. They have tiny pockets, or bladders, on their underwater leaves and stems. Each bladder has a trap-door which it keeps closed until a water-flea or other tiny animal brushes against it. Then it swings open and the creature is sucked inside and digested.

Which plants smell like meat?

Here you can see a Rafflesia arnoldii flower in Sumatra.

Some plants smell like rotting meat to attract flies for pollination (see pages 20 and 22). They include the Rafflesia, which has the biggest and, perhaps, the smelliest flower in the world. Its terrible stink attracts swarms of flies, who think they are in for a tasty meal

of meat. Instead, they fly away covered in pollen. Stapelia flowers smell almost as bad. They also look like chunks of rotting meat to fool the flies even more.

Which plants live off other plants?

Plants such as mistletoe and dodders steal food and water from other living plants. These 'thieves' are called parasites. They climb and twist up another plant's roots or stems. As they climb, they send out hundreds of tiny suckers which look a bit like roots. These force their way into the plant's own food and water tubes, and suck out the goodness and moisture.

Mistletoe grows on oak and apple trees. It is only partly a parasite as it can also make its own food. In some countries, people think that mistletoe is magical. It is cut and used for lucky charms.

Mistletoe sometimes grows around tree-trunks.

How do trees grow?

Each year a tree grows bigger. Its trunk and branches grow longer and thicker to support the tree's extra weight. The roots spread further underground to anchor the tree more firmly and take in more water.

The tree's trunk and branches grow fatter because a new layer of wood grows each year, under the bark. This new layer is called sapwood. It is soft, living wood, carrying food and water around the tree. The older wood in the centre of the trunk is called heartwood. It is hard and dead. Its job is to support the trunk, as a steel girder, or beam, supports a building. Almost all the wood in a tree-trunk is dead heartwood.

How can you tell the age of a tree?

A tree's new layer of sapwood grows in a ring shape. By counting these rings on a cut tree-trunk, you can find out how old this tree was. If you go for a walk in a wood or forest, look out for a fallen tree and count its **annual** rings.

You can also tell what the weather might have been like in the past, by looking at a cut tree-trunk. Wide rings only grow when there is plenty of rain. Narrow rings form in dry years. Trees grow quickest of all in the spring when the weather is warm but still damp.

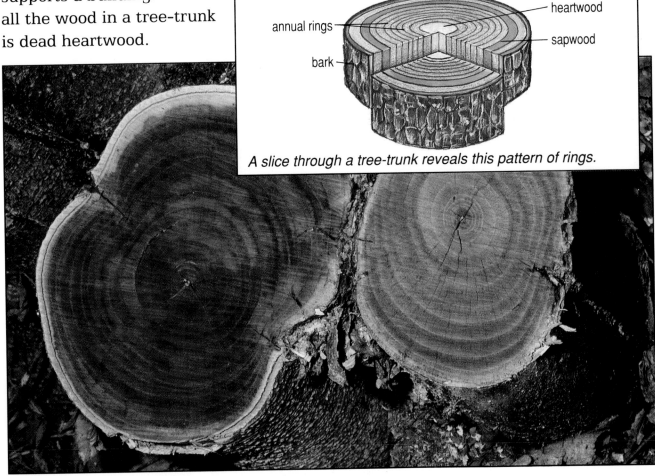

annual rings — heartwood — sapwood — bark

A slice through a tree-trunk reveals this pattern of rings.

You can see the annual rings clearly in these two tree-trunk sections.

The tallest tree in the world is a coast redwood tree growing in California, USA. It is 113.7 metres tall. This is over 80 times taller than you are.

A coast redwood in California towers into the sky.

The heaviest wood comes from the black ironwood tree. Balsa is one of the lightest types of wood. It would take ten buckets of balsa wood to weigh as much as one bucket of water. It would take 15 buckets of balsa to weigh as much as one bucket of black ironwood.

This is what a coast redwood branch and its cones look like.

See for yourself

You can work out how old a tree is without having to cut it down and count its growth rings. Most trees grow about 2.5 centimetres thicker each year. Measure around a tree-trunk about 1.5 metres above the ground. This measurement is the tree's **circumference**. Now divide the circumference by 2.5 centimetres to give you the tree's age. For example, if the tree's circumference is 125 centimetres, then the tree is 50 years old (125 divided by 2.5 = 50).

Children measuring a redwood tree.

Why do trees have bark?

The dead, outer covering of a tree-trunk is called bark. It is very tough. The main job of bark is to protect the tree-trunk from attack by animals such as squirrels, deer, birds and insects. Bark also protects the tree from diseases spread by fungi (see pages 42 and 43), and the weather. It stops the tree from drying out, and **insulates** it from very hot or very cold weather.

The bark of this tree has been broken by a green woodpecker to make his nest hole.

Without its bark 'skin', the tree would not be able to grow. The delicate tubes carrying food and water around the tree lie just under the bark. If they are damaged, the tree may die. Tiny holes in the bark, called lenticels, allow the tree to breathe.

Why does bark make different patterns?

Because it is dead, the bark cannot stretch as the tree-trunk grows thicker and fatter. So it cracks, splits and peels, making the different patterns which you can see. Each type of tree has its own special bark pattern. Old oak trees have deep cracks and grooves in their bark. Birch trees have bark which peels off in strips. The strips are paper-thin, but so tough and waterproof that North American Indians once used them to cover their canoes. Pine trees and other conifers tend to have flaky bark. Many young trees have smooth bark that gets more patterned as the trees get older.

Oak.

Silver birch.

Scots pine.

The patterns on different types of bark can be very smooth or quite rough and cracked.

Where does cork come from?

Cork is the bark of the cork-oak tree. The bark is so thick that it can be stripped off without hurting the tree. A new layer of bark soon grows again. Cork can absorb moisture, is slightly elastic and can protect things from heat. This is why we use it to make bottle corks, floor tiles and table mats.

 Did you know?

The bark on a beech tree is only about 1 centimetre thick. But the bark on a redwood tree may be 30 times as thick.

 Did you know?

A tree in Hawaii has bark that is specially designed to protect the tree from the red-hot ashes and cinders which erupt from nearby volcanoes.

Rolls of cork-oak bark have been stripped off a cork-oak tree like the one above.

! See for yourself

You should never peel or strip the bark off a tree. But you can make bark rubbings to keep a record of the different types of bark which you see. Tape a sheet of strong, white paper to a tree trunk. Then rub gently over it with a soft, thick wax crayon until the bark pattern shows through. Write down the name of the tree on each rubbing.

This is how to make a bark rubbing.

How do plants protect themselves?

Plants cannot run away from danger, so they need other ways of protecting themselves from harm. They need defences from animals that attack them for food, and they need protection from the weather. Plants have many clever methods of self-defence, including the use of weapons such as thorns, prickles and poisons.

Holly leaves have double protection. They have shiny, waxy coats to stop them from drying out in the cold wind. They also have prickly leaves to stop animals from eating them. Next time you see a holly bush, look closely at the difference between the upper leaves and those near the bottom. The leaves near the bottom are much more prickly because they are most at risk from animals.

Some plants contain deadly poisons that can put off even the hungriest animals. Many fungi are highly poisonous (see pages 42 and 43). If someone eats a death-cap toadstool it can kill them. Foxglove leaves also contain poisons which can damage the heart. However, they can be used in very tiny amounts to help cure heart diseases.

Above: A holly bush has shiny green leaves and bright red berries.
Right: The Clouded clitocybe fungus growing among the grass can cause stomach pains.

How do plants survive the cold?

Plants growing in cold places such as the slopes of high mountains, or at the Arctic and Antarctic, face two main problems. They need ways of coping with the freezing cold and the biting winds.

The edelweiss plant grows on the slopes of the Alps in Europe. Its flowers and leaves are hairy. This helps it to trap warmth from the sun, and stops it from drying out in the wind. Another Alpine plant, the Alpine snowbell, has an even more unusual way of surviving. It makes and gives out enough heat to melt a tiny area of snow around it, so that it can grow in the frozen ground.

Many mountain plants grow close to the ground, in thick clumps, to keep warm and out of the wind. In some places, trees such as dwarf willows and pines would barely reach your knees.

Beautiful gentians grow in the French Alps.

Which plant has collapsing leaves?

The mimosa plant has an unusual way of stopping insects from eating its leaves. They collapse, all of a sudden, just seconds after an insect lands on them. This helps to shake an insect off, but it also puts off larger animals such as deer. These animals take one look at the wilted, collapsed leaves and set off in search of something more appetising. The mimosa's leaves also collapse when the weather is cold. At night they fold up into a 'sleeping' position. No one is sure why this happens, but it has earned the mimosa the nickname 'sensitive plant'.

A mimosa has open leaves when it is left undisturbed.

The mimosa's leaves collapse when they are touched.

Which plants glow in the dark?

Dinoflagellates are tiny sea plants with just one cell. They are so small that usually they can only be seen under a microscope. But they often form large groups in warm places such as the Indian Ocean. The amazing thing about these plants is that they glow in the dark. Each plant makes a tiny amount of light, and the whole group makes the surface of the water shimmer and sparkle. The light from some very large groups is so good that you could read a book by it.

Some types of jungle fungi also make their own light. They glow green, white or yellow. No one knows for certain why they do this. It may be a means of protection from hungry beetles and other insects. If these insects were lit up, they would be seen too easily by their own enemies.

Above: *A fungus glowing on the jungle floor.*
Inset: *You can see the glow given out by this magnified dinoflagellate.*

Passion-flower vines have very odd leaves. They have strange growths on them, shaped like butterfly eggs. These stop butterflies from laying their real eggs on the leaves. In this way, the false eggs protect the leaves from hungry caterpillars which would have hatched out.

You can see the false eggs underneath this passion-flower leaf.

butterfly egg growths

Which plants look like pebbles?

Some plants use clever disguises to hide themselves from hungry animals. Stone plants live in the deserts of South Africa. They grow on stony ground. Their swollen leaves look so much like pebbles that animals pass them by. The leaves are even coloured mottled brown, grey and white like the real stones around them. This type of disguise is called camouflage. It is only obvious that these 'stones' are plants when their brightly-coloured flowers appear.

Can you tell which are the plants and which are the pebbles?

Lichens in Antarctica survive by growing very slowly indeed. Their slow growth saves their energy for coping with the harsh weather conditions. These lichens would take about 100 years to reach the size of your thumbnail.

Lichens growing in Antarctica.

How can desert plants live without water?

All plants need some water to live, even if it is only a small amount. In the desert, however, water is very scarce. Plants have to struggle to find enough moisture to survive. Some have very clever ways of doing this.

Cacti grow mainly in the deserts of North America. They store water in their thick stems and use it during the long desert droughts. On a rare rainy day, a large cactus can take in up to a tonne of water. The stems of these plants sometimes have pleats running down them, which allow the stems to stretch as they fill with water.

Cacti belong to a group of plants called succulents. Many succulents also have fleshy leaves that can store water. Others store water in their roots. Succulents have tough, waxy 'skins' to stop water from escaping. Some cacti are covered in fine, white 'wool' which also cuts down water loss and helps to keep the plant cool.

Other desert plants have similar ways of getting enough water to survive. Baobab trees store water in their trunks. These swell up as they fill, and then shrink as the tree uses up the water supply. Creosote bushes have a huge network of shallow roots that stretches over a large area of ground, collecting any drops of moisture, however small.

These three types of cactus are different shapes but they are all thick and fleshy.
Far left: *Saguaro cactus.*
Above: *Prickly pear cactus.*
Left: *Barrel cactus.*

Why do cacti have spines?

Cactus spines are actually leaves. In this prickly form, these leaves can protect the plant against hungry or thirsty animals. They also help to cut down water loss. Large leaves lose a lot of water through their stomata (see page 19). So cacti have developed thin, sharp spines instead of leaves. These lose very little water. Some cactus spines may be up to 15 centimetres long.

Top: Cactus spines lose little water.
Above: Large, open leaves lose a lot of water.

Why do some deserts suddenly burst into flower?

In the desert it may be months, or even years, between one fall of rain and the next. So plants have to make the most of any downpour. When it rains, some desert plants such as desert peas, poppies, sand verbenas and sunflowers can grow, flower and make seeds very quickly indeed. This is when the desert suddenly bursts into bloom. Afterwards, the flower seeds lie in the ground until the next rainfall, which may be many months away.

After rain, the desert bursts into bloom.

? Did you know?

The biggest cacti of all are the giant saguaros which grow in the USA and Mexico. They can stand over 17 metres tall and weigh 10 tonnes, as much as three rhinoceroses. An amazing 9 tonnes of the weight is water stored in the huge stems of these cacti.

! See for yourself

Try to make your own mini desert and grow some cacti in it. Fill a large, shallow clay flowerpot or box with a mixture of sand and potting compost. Plant a few small cacti and cover the surface with a layer of gravel or small stones. Keep your cacti in a warm, sunny place. They only need watering a little in winter.

What is seaweed?

Seaweed belongs to the group of plants called algae. Many algae are tiny plants that are made of only one cell. They are simple plants with no flowers, proper leaves or stems. Algae can live almost anywhere – on tree-trunks, in ponds and in the sea. Seaweeds are the biggest types of algae. Some can grow over 65 metres long. They grow along rocky shores, or float on the surface of the water, held up by air-filled 'bladders' on their strands. They cannot live deeper down because there is not enough light for photosynthesis (see page 10).

Seaweeds living along the shore often have thick suckers, called holdfasts, at their bases. The holdfasts anchor the plants so that they are not washed away by the tides.

In some countries, such as Japan and Ireland, seaweed is harvested like any other crop. It has many uses as food, as fertilizer for crops, and to make shampoo, toothpaste and even ice-cream.

Above: Oarweed floats in the sea at low tide.
Inset: The bladders on seaweed strands are full of air.

Which plants can forecast the weather?

Seaweeds are supposed to be able to help you to forecast the weather. If you hang a piece of seaweed by the window, it should dry out if hot weather is on the way, and become softer if wetter weather is coming.

Other plant forecasters include pine cones. A cone contains a pine tree's seeds. In warm, dry weather the cone's scales open up to let the seeds fall out. This is because the seeds will survive better in this type of weather. But the cones remain tightly closed if the weather is bad.

A Virginia pine cone opens all its scales in the warm weather.

 Did you know?

Algae can turn snow red. In 1818, the explorer, John Ross, reported seeing large areas of red snow in the Arctic. Very few people believed his story. But he was telling the truth. Patches of crimson-red snow are caused by huge numbers of tiny, one-celled algae called Protococci.

Which plants can test pollution?

You might have seen orange or green patches of lichen growing on walls or rocks. A lichen is a very odd plant, made up of a mixture of two other plants – an alga and a fungus (see pages 7, 8 and 42). The two plants work as partners. The alga makes food for the fungus by photosynthesis. The fungus provides water for the alga and holds the whole plant firmly down.

Lichens are very sensitive to air pollution. Have a look around the area where you live. How many lichens are growing there? What colour are they? Are they leafy or crusty? If the air is very dirty, no lichens will grow. If the air is very clean, you should find some leafy green lichens. You may only be able to see these lichens in the countryside.

Thick crusts of lichens grow on rocks by the sea.

What are fungi?

Fungi are such strange plants that some botanists do not count them as plants at all. Fungi have no proper roots or stems. They have no leaves or flowers and do not make seeds. They cannot make their own food because they do not contain any chlorophyll. So how do fungi grow and what do they eat?

Instead of seeds, fungi produce millions of microscopic spores, which are like tiny specks of dust. These are blown far from the parent plant by the wind. If the spores land in a suitable place, they grow into new fungi.

The part of a fungus which you see above the ground is called its 'fruiting body'. But this is only about a tenth of the fungus. The whole fungus is made up of tiny threads, called hyphae. Some of these are woven together to make the fruiting body. Many more run underground or into tree-trunks and other surfaces.

The threads take in food from dead and living plants or animals. Fungi live off rotting fruit, dead leaves and even human beings. Skin diseases such as athlete's foot and ringworm are caused by fungi. Fungi also make bread and fruit go mouldy.

Left above: *Chanterelle*
Left: *Puffball*
Above: *Fly agaric*

Fungi come in all shapes, size and colours.
Never *pick wild fungi to eat.*

What is the difference between mushrooms and toadstools?

Fungi come in many shapes and sizes. Some are flat and plate-shaped, and grow out of tree-trunks. Giant puffballs are quite round, as their name suggests. Others look like ears. But the most common fungi are mushroom-shaped, with a stalk topped by an umbrella-shaped cap.

Mushrooms belong to the group of fungi known as toadstools. But we usually talk about mushrooms when we really mean the kinds of toadstools which we can eat. Many toadstools are very poisonous indeed. If you see mushrooms or toadstools in the wild, do not pick them to eat. It is often very difficult to tell if they are poisonous or not. If you touch fungi, always wash your hands afterwards.

 Did you know?

The death-cap is the most poisonous fungus in the world. It can kill a person in just six hours.

Above: Death caps such as these are deadly.
Left: Parasol mushrooms are edible but look dangerously like death caps.

 See for yourself

You can look more closely at a mushroom's spores by making a spore print from a mushroom that you have bought in a shop. Cut the stem off the fresh, smooth mushroom. The spores grow on ridges under the cap. If the mushroom has white ridges, you will need a piece of dark paper. If it has dark ridges, you will need light paper. Place the cap on the paper and leave it overnight. Then lift the cap very carefully and look at the spore print which it has left behind. Do not tilt the paper or the print will fall off.

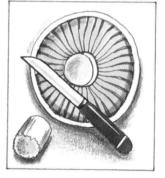

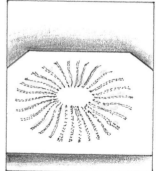

How do people use plants?

Have a quick glance around your bedroom or classroom. How many things can you see that are made of plants? There may be wooden furniture, newspapers, books or magazines. Most of the timber which is used to make furniture comes from conifers. It is called softwood because it is usually easier to cut. Wood from conifers is also used to make paper (see opposite). Timber from broad-leaved trees is called hardwood. It is usually much tougher. Do you play a musical instrument? Violins and guitars are made mainly from wood. The black keys on a piano are often made from a hardwood called ebony.

Now what about your clothes? Are you wearing anything made of cotton? Cotton is made from the fine white threads which grow around the seeds of cotton plants.

This room has many objects that are made from plants. How many can you find?

But the kitchen is the place where you will see most plants. Animals and people depend on plants for nourishment. This is because plants can make their own food and therefore are a food store for other living things. We eat some plants directly, such as fruit, vegetables, rice, wheat and so on. Some of us also eat meat from cows and sheep which once fed on grass. So in fact we are eating the grass ourselves, but only indirectly. This series of links is called a food chain. There are a lot different food chains involving many different animals. But there is a plant at the beginning of every one.

We also flavour our food with herbs and spices, which are themselves plants, or parts of plants. Cinnamon spice, for example, comes from the bark of the cinnamon tree. Many medicines also come from plants. The rosy periwinkle from Madagascar, for example, has been used to treat people suffering from leukaemia (cancer of the blood). It has been more successful than any other treatment tried before.

These are just some of the ways in which people use plants. Can you think of any more?

 Did you know?

Some trees make a milky sap called latex. It can be very useful. Chewing-gum is made from the latex of the chicle tree, which grows in Central America. Rubber is made from the latex of the rubber tree.

How is paper made?

Paper is made from the wood of conifers, such as spruce and pine trees. Wood chips are mixed with water and special chemicals. They are 'cooked' until the mixture is very soft. At this stage the mixture is called pulp. Then it is washed and mashed to break up any remaining fragments of wood. The pulp is then put into a machine that squeezes any water out, leaving the paper behind. This is dried and wound into rolls.

The first paper-like material was made about 2,500 years ago by the Ancient Egyptians. It was called papyrus. It was made from mashed and pulped papyrus reeds.

Papyrus grows along Lake Naivasha in Kenya.

Glossary

absorbs takes in, or soaks up

adapted changed over a long period of time to suit different conditions or environments

annual yearly; something that happens every year

bleached made lighter in colour

cell the smallest living thing; the building block from which all living things are made

circumference the measurement around the edge of a circle or a round object

digestive juices juices inside an animal or plant which help to break down food into parts that the animal or plant can use

environments the rocks, buildings, trees and other plants among which a plant grows

fronds leaves, especially ferns and palms

identify to find out the name or type of something

insulates protects, usually against the cold or the heat

microscopic something that can only be seen in detail with the help of a microscope

nourishing foods containing a lot of goodness, which keeps animals and plants healthy

nutrients minerals, vitamins and other good things in food: they help animals and plants to grow and stay healthy

parallel lines running next to each other, but never touching; they are separated by the same distance all along their length; railway tracks are a good example

potting compost a special mixture of soil and broken-down, rotted plant and animal matter; it is good for the healthy growth of flowers and vegetables that are planted in it

spores special single cells that can reproduce, or make new plants, on their own, without needing any other cells

water vapour water in the air in the form of an invisible gas

Books to read

Ecology Watch (Evan Brothers)
    Rainforests Rodney Aldis
    Grasslands Alan Colinson
Eyewitness Guides (Dorling Kindersley)
    Plants David Burnie
    Trees David Burnie
Focus on Trees Anita Ganeri (Franklin Watts)
Nature Detective Plants Anita Ganeri (Franklin Watts)
Green Inheritance Anthony Huxley (Gaia Books)
The Plants Life Nature Library (Time Life)
Last Frontiers for Mankind (Evans Brothers)
    Jungles Lawrence Williams